PRAISE FOR
POST-APOCALYPTIC VALENTINE

"I have loved everything I've ever read by Linda Watanabe McFerrin. Her prose and poetry are filled with amazing women, charm, wisdom, and light. She is both soulful and precise, eloquent and full of life."
—**Anne Lamott, author of** *Bird by Bird* **and** *Hallelujah, Anyway*

"Some poets just bring you joy. Some poets just make you hear thoughts never thought before,with ways of saying them so new— It rocks the page. There's heartbreak enough in *POST-Apocalyptic Valentine*, ecological worries too, tragedies and deaths, rough stuff for women; but Linda Watanabe McFerrin just makes you happy to read her jaunty life-giving version of it. The work is smart, sometimes sassy, and that's the appeal. Beneath the line there's an hydraulic of good spirit—the pleasure of making art—that seeps through. A few poems in collaboration with Erin Orison are particularly interesting, where two voices are   as one; also, there's ekphrastic poetry where you don't even want the painting, the poem is sensual enough. This is a book to own, not only for its intelligence and emotional agility, but for so much new truth to be had. In one poem McFerrin praises Dylan Thomas, saying, "I crawl through the belly/ of syllables..." Well, we do too, here in this book, with the deepest possible enjoyment."
—**Grace Cavalieri, Maryland's tenth Poet Laureate**

"Haunted by history as well as by present ghosts, ghouls, and goblins, Watanabe's poems are charged with the force of the great changes we're facing—as a planet, as a society, and as individuals. And yet their ferocity is tempered with a gracious attention to the delicate details of daily life—these are poems that listen even more loudly than they speak, and that generosity gives this collection its distinctively heart-felt edge—it's a tour de force of compassion."
—**Cole Swensen, author of** *And And And,* **longlisted for the Griffin Poetry Prize**

POST-APOCALYPTIC VALENTINE

by

Linda Watanabe McFerrin

7.13 Books
Brooklyn

ALSO BY LINDA WATANABE MCFERRIN

The Impossibility of Redemption Is Something We Hadn't Figured On
Namako, Sea Cucumber
The Hand of Buddha
Dead Love
Navigating the Divide

Printed in the United States of America

First Edition
1 2 3 4 5 6 7 8 9

Cover art by Gigi Little
Cover photo by Lowry McFerrin
Cover image "Free Love Phone Booth" by Iröndäd
Poetry Edited by James Cihlar

Library of Congress Cataloging-in-Publication Data

ISBN (paperback): 979-8-9891214-6-5
ISBN (eBook): 979-8-9891214-7-2

CONTENTS

ON PLUTO (cont'd)

FOREWORD
BY JAMES CIHLAR

"I BELIEVE IN GHOSTS, although I have never seen them," Linda Watanabe McFerrin writes in *POST-Apocalyptic Valentine*, a book that, paradoxically, is filled with zombies, ninjas, witches, and yes, ghosts. However, McFerrin's fifth volume is unapologetically a book about the body, our corporeal existence: "Do we simply tweak and jump/ as anything would/ when infused by a charge?" ("The Brain, the Body, and His Arms.")

This book cheekily explores the body's lusts and indiscretions, because, "let's face it,/ we're all whores./ We do it to get paid." Some of the poems are co-signed by Erin Orison, the sensual/supernatural protagonist of *Dead Love*, McFerrin's cross-genre zombie/philosophical novel. A series of ekphrastic poems on sculptures serve as a sort of chorus, adding another layer to the book's contemplation of physicality. *POST-Apocalyptic Valentine* presents a world of longings, allegiances, and appetites—familial and sensual, individual and corporate, where even "This Sunset" is a "bloody barbecue," because the sky itself is poisoned with byproducts.

If such commentary brings "Moloch" to mind, the reader may be forgiven, as McFerrin herself is a latter-day poet of the Bay Area, a location she shares with Ginsberg, and a place pivotal in American consciousness and in world art and culture. Those familiar with

I

McFerrin's travel writing will not be surprised at the metropolitan, cosmopolitan tone of this book; she moves through the dark and bright of the world, notating ethereal and passing loveliness in lucid imagery, a literary cousin to Audrey Hepburn as Holly Golightly. Trains are a recurrent motif, with vivid imagery of motion ("night . . . begins to pocket about me"), encapsulating the perambulatory nature of the book itself, underscoring the theme of the transitory, temporal passage of the body.

In some ways, *POST-Apocalyptic Valentine* is a welcome, Feminist update of Allen Ginsberg's "Howl." Prophecies such as "What Every Girl Should Know" urge us to recognize the damage we have done to the planet and acknowledge the regret we feel for what we have bequeathed to later generations. In "Denial," the aftermath of an earthquake is a metaphor for environmental degradation: "the black sky,/ chipped away in pieces,/ was a furious red/ where the Marina burned/ sullenly." The poem title "Three Movements" puns on earthquakes while the poem's lines allude to both our shared emergence from a world pandemic—"Even now, when we/ are gingerly climbing back into/ our lives"—as well as to the memory of personal loss and the contemplation of mortality: "None of the clocks is really keeping time."

The immediacy and originality of the imagery in these poems is complemented by disarmingly oracular pronouncements. In "Is Invisible," a suppressed childhood memory of a father's affair leading to the firing of a pregnant maid reminds the poet of the loss of her infant daughter: "we both died at thirty/ the rest of our lives being spent as ghosts." The ode "For Bert," a friend who passed of AIDS in the late eighties, is moving due to its emotional restraint, providing the only moment of stasis in this otherwise processional book: "In a way, the world has stopped moving."

"None of the myths is really true," McFerrin writes in "Is Invisible," yet their traces are woven through these pages. As within her fiction, including *Namako: Sea Cucumber* and *The Hand of Buddha*, here the notion of kami is important. These objects of worship in Shintō religion straddle the gray area between nature and divinity, good and evil, living comfortably in both/all realms. McFerrin's poems explode the Western assumption that one thing can be true at a time, persuading us instead that "the dead are surviving the living."

–James Cihlar, PhD
author of *The Shadowgraph*
(University of New Mexico Press, 2020)

POST-APOCALYPTIC
VALENTINE

Dark Parent

The ninja knows
that the shadows provide
the shelter you seek
but recoil from,
being beige,
perhaps pastel,
a target, actually ...

knows
that you will break cover
because "sneak"
and "lurk" are
bad words
to you

knows you will streak
into the sunlight
where the brilliance
will halo your
dark form

because you are heavy and slow
and human
and do not love the void—
your dark parent—
the only thing
that can shield you.

—Linda Watanabe McFerrin/Erin Orison

What Every Girl Should Know

Every girl should read the books that boys read,
see that war and machinery are in their future,
that the soft flesh will melt in the blast furnace of invention,
that the old patterns will be laughed at, passé.
New creations mean new variations on a cold and metallic theme.
Oh, masterful manipulation, we salute your direction,
and at night, when it is black-out and all the hearth-fires dead,
we chalk in imaginary lines between the distant constellations,
hoping that one day the scrap we are left with
will take us to the stars.

—Linda Watanabe McFerrin/Erin Orison

A Ghost Reflects on the Ninja

That night when the frogs were singing,
the nightingale floor went wild,
its creak-tweet warning us
of trouble in tabi afoot.

No one ignored it,
but we were too slow.
Assassins entered our bedrooms,
ushering in death.

It is true their swords, like water,
reflected the lanterns' false moonlight,
but we knew it was darkness that skewered us,
our throats smiling in silence
as the shadows leaked in
and the frogs continued to sing.

—Linda Watanabe McFerrin/Erin Orison

Note: The "nightingale floor" in Nijo Castle was laid to guard against intrusion by suspicious and dangerous ninja assassins. Suspended above the frame with the aid of special iron clamps, the floor moved up and down over the fixing nails when walked upon, creating a sound similar to the song of a nightingale.

Witches

You who are young and not so plump,
inedible really, like that boy, Hansel,
who was so insolent—
how could you *not* want to cage him
and taunt him with the daily measurement?
The chicken bone trick fooled no one.
But you, the girl, showed promise:
working away, resentful,
bearing your secret grudge,
using your wiles. Yes, the wiles make a witch.
We do not want the dumb ones.
You must count and remember
and never forget the good or the bad.
You must keep it
stored in a jar in a dark, quiet place,
like your mind or the cabinet of
memory.
Shun us at your peril.
We will turn you into one of us.
This is no spell.
It's a promise.
Yes, this is a promise.

—Linda Watanabe McFerrin/Erin Orison

Train

The train
at sunset seems
endless—
stretches out of
the coral light,
oxide hide
rusty
like an old accordion—
container, container, container.
I wait at the crossing
while night descends,
begins to pocket about me.
The rail cars bulge
efficiently,
flash past my face,
their surfaces a red gash
zooming toward
a different and inexplicable
horizon.

This Sunset

In this bloody barbeque of a sunset
gulls sweep over the salt sea,
where it has turned pink—
a chemical pink, not like flamingos,
like cobalt chloride or manganese salts.
There is a smell in the air like sulfides,
the lake has a head on it—foaming and poisonous—
and the skies brood over us, a simmering cauldron—
red at night, yellow madder by day.

The Almond Grove

Fresno, California 1986

For four years I have been gnashing over
the bitterness of almonds.
You know: that Fresno morning
in the cold grove, after we had stuffed ourselves
on the unripe nuts.
Our mouths met in a kiss
limed in acrid surprise.

I have been combing metaphors
for what I thought was lyrical.
Some moments are epiphanous.
Some cast themselves
in harder lines.

That was the morning when we saw
the cow lying bloated in a field,
its four legs, stiff as clothespins,
pointed toward heaven.
The other cows gave it a wide berth,
settled across the yard,
silently munching old grass.

That odd death—
I had thought to exclude it—
is somehow fitting,
like the rain-soaked almond husks
decaying, collapsing when our thumbs
pushed through them,
or the clean white teeth
of the almond meat.

Foot in Mouth
Shanghai, 2010

The chickens' feet sit
in a mountain
like hands larger
than an infant's
and shiny.
My sister smiles
on the other side
of the pile.
"You aren't going to eat that,"
she threatens.
"I am," I say,
nibbling at
the slick fat
that wraps around
the bony metatarsals.
"To throw them out
is a waste."

I taste vinegar,
the opposite of joy,
imagine chickens
going footless
to the market.

When I have eaten
two feet
my sister says,
"You wouldn't eat calves' balls
would you?"
I toy with one more chicken foot.
I feel like throwing up.
"Yeah," I say.
—that's why I *love* this girl—
"Wouldn't you?"

—Linda Watanabe McFerrin/Erin Orison

Kato

Kato, you are my mystery, boy.
I think
you are a green poison,
seeping into his bones,
giving him everything he needs

—Linda Watanabe McFerrin/Erin Orison

Is Love a Dumpster Dive?

I love bad boys,
not the kind that behave badly,
but the ones gone bad,
the rotten ones.

Dig in. Dig in.

Sometimes you find perfection
—or very nearly—
something, someone
to get you through
a bad night,
another day,
a lifetime.

Sometimes ...
the whole thing
makes you sick.

But you have to eat,
right?
Well, the rotten ones
are free.

—Linda Watanabe McFerrin/Erin Orison

Absinthe

So, the long finger of envy
twisted a ghoulish digit
toward me:
How do I hate thee?
Let me count the ways,
the days
between me and the revenge
I will take
like a sword flying out.

Green goblin,
see what you do to me?
Counting what's due to me,
it's you I hate
like a light going out.

The Brain, the Body, and His Arms

Consider that pink-grey thing
ponderously calculating,
pushing its formulas
across universes,
game-pieces over wide, black tables
that slide into other planes,
rolling a pair
of mathematical dice,
translating the metaphors
in rutilated crystals
into long syntactical ribbons.

Imagine a sense a humor,
this projection, merely,
onto the pink-grey mass.
Its dense ruminations
are unamused.

Are wide eyes and smiles,
is laughter
only a thing of the body—
no more than the semaphores
of messages
from neurons and synapses
excited
by the movement
of some new piece of information
along
their length,
tin cans joined by a taut piece of string?
Do we simply tweak and jump
as anything would
when infused by a charge,
a cat or a dog, for example,
transmogrified by
an electric current?
Are these twitches so varied?

We have come so close to love.
But his arms remain
calipers,
measuring his reactions,
and mine.

At 4 p.m.

No one told you that
at four o'clock in the afternoon
you would no longer be important,
that you would be moving into shadow—
not even you can sustain any interest
in this person in need of tucks and tacking—

that you would not be the person
they want to see in the morning
but the last thing they want to see at night.

POST-Apocalyptic Valentine

My heart, my love,
FRAGILE
was on the line
HANDLE WITH CARE
when everything went haywire.
CONTENTS MAY SHIFT UNDER PRESSURE
You, a zombie now,
CONTENTS MAY SPILL UNDER PRESSURE
without a clue about me
or you—
promises all broken and
an apocalypse looming ...
URGENT
URGENT
URGENT
I need to send a bullet
SPECIAL DELIVERY
into your brain.
EXPRESS MAIL
I am so sorry.
RETURN TO SENDER
ADDRESSEE UNKNOWN

—Linda Watanabe McFerrin/Erin Orison

Grandma

She has come, you say,
with two sake cups.
I can only think of the stories,
the stories you haven't yet
shared with me

about Canton—the way they took
old Ross away,
confiscated the house,
and you fled.

He died in a camp
while you angled for
a haven in the land of your
father.

Yellow-white half-cast,
they set you adrift on a
war-torn ocean of drama,
in a whirlpool of misery.
Now your mama is back
with the rice wine.
Kampai!
The dead are surviving the living.

I am jealous, not just for the visit,
for the company, for the booze,
for your sisterhood,
for the stories.

Romance

I had imagined her upon a hill,
half-clad, the breeze between her legs.

I am a passenger in the car.
The car is going nowhere.

Once, I saw her in a rowboat,
drifting out to that little island
way out in the bay.

There are certain details about my job
that torment me.

She is always in some vast and open space,
abstracted and remote.

Last night I had a dream in which the rats
finally eat the man's face.

Yesterday, the dress she wore was white,
her shoes the same color as cream.

The man was hanging from a pendulum,
and the pendulum dropped, as it does
in some big clocks at the prescribed hour
(while the spring rewinds),
before it begins its climb again toward
the future.

Vitrines

IV 1964/78

Substanz I und substanz II
schokolade
catkins honig or kelp
petrification
meringue-filled shit
und
old empires from Munchen
Lowenbrau
a dirty hive
or honey smear
at the bunched
root
of wheat sheaves.

Coyotes

The coyotes wait for me beside the screen door.
They are yellow,
and that is the color of death.
Fireflies buzz
on the other side of the screen.
The lawn and the sidewalk
settle into darkness.
The coyotes' fur
is yellow and short,
and their bright eyes,
like headlamps,
are yellow also,
and that is the color of death.
I have run out of chicken.
I have run out of milk.
Even the stars have closed
their doors.
The coyotes wait for me
on the other side of the screen.
They are yellow.

Turnstyle: the Clean New Future

after a painting by Roberto Matta
l'entree d l'acte, 1961

Trumpet
engine
"interieur"
some kind of geometric
crystals
the diffuse green
occasional levers
cylinders
evocation of horsepower
a wild lurch forward
as evinced by
vestigal numbers
a number of erasures
somewhat mystical
as paint is simply layered over
citrus colors find their way into the landscape
sharp discs spinning
the blunt nose of a craft
thrust toward center
a buoyant optimism
a smell like oranges
and Pine-sol

Bolinas

I want to be in Bolinas
when the world ends,
watch this pearl of a planet
swallowed by the nacreous
crepuscular
swell of sky
coming clean,
going dark as
night.

Black

Black Sabbath, black as night, blackout, blackamoor, black at'cha, to hell and black, blacklist, black beauty, black is back, black light, black buster, black gammon, black cat, black foot, black belt, black, black, black,
black off.

HEART BREAK

A Love Story

She has a large heart.
Her heart is in her mouth.
Her heart is on her sleeve.
Her heart is bleeding.
Her heart is broken.
She has lost her heart.

She is like a bunraku puppet.

He has stolen her heart.
Her heart has taken a beating.
She listens to her heart.
Her heart is her guide.
Her heart is empty.

She is like a bunraku puppet.

Her heart aches.
Everything gives her heartburn.
They are talking heart to heart.
It is a heartless place.

She is like a bunraku puppet.

Puppet master in black,
moving this way and that,
he sets things in motion, unseen.

She has come to the heart of the matter.
She has followed her heart.
We have seen into her heart.
A black heart.
A sorrowful heart.
The heart offended.
A dark, dark heart.

She is like a bunraku puppet.
She is like a bunraku puppet.
She is like a bunraku puppet.

Note: Bunraku - a form of Japanese puppet theater in which puppeteers dress in black, and visible to the audience, manipulate large puppets to the accompaniment of chanted narration and musical instruments.

Reveille

Shshshsh.
You are frozen,
listening,
and the animal moves beneath you,
articulating,
haunches gathering,
uncurling
in the singeing early morning frost
where the forest meets the railroad tracks,
but the snap of twigs
like rifle-shot in the empty air
seems far,
almost on ice.
Some part of you, similarly,
is unaware
of how the black twigs snap back into your face
or the hushed chill about you
      only the line where you and the animal meet
      and the movement rotates,
      filling your limbs,
      fluid.
This is excruciating,
the way your chest is arabesqueing,
stretching across the thin crack
of dawn
unsure, this footing on ice,
but the movement is
forward is
breaking is
is . . . is . . . is.
Icicles melt
and the forest hisses like a train.

Night Train

South of France 1988

on the night train from Paris
the railroad car swings on its carriage,
a wild soul careening along its earthly track.
Vampiric night floods the compartment—
dark shift of landscape,
fields rush by,
shadowy flowers.
The swing of the creaky couchettes,
the dark grip of a tunnel,
the face of the woman across from me,
ghoulish and sleeping,
a big wax apple
muffled in blankets,
my own white cheek on the pillow,
our dreams tossed in the tight darkness like soft balls of wax—
we sleep, or try to,
sarcophagi,
fixed granitelike neighbors,
bodies laid out in a crypt—
rickety silence/rickety noise
rickety silence/rickety noise
rickety silence.

For Bert

Bert died of AIDS in 1988.

I.
It is odd,
or is it only
the angle, the way it reflects—
smaller and somehow
smaller—
like muscle exhaustion, the
way
you are relaxing away from us?
Or is it we who are drifting?

You, shining,
in the way of
an object newly placed,
having that halo of wholeness had only
by completed acts.

Your kisses
are walking on eggshells.

Have we all become
cubes and spheres merely,
an inarticulate landscape abiding
by its subsets of rules?
You are the object passing out of my realm
as I am passing out of yours.
You have your own requirements,
things insistent as breath.
A myopic haze settles over you—
diffuse but separate—
as something fading out of view.
I am astounded by the quietness:
a silent room, the furniture

draped in sheets,
the mantelpiece is littered with
old photos of friends.
I watch you arranging flowers
or simply
getting a drink, the tap-water running
into the glass.
And your patience arrests me.

You are slipping away through
my fingers. Each embrace
smaller until
you are a mouse, silent and brown with
very dark eyes,
the delicate heave of your chest
unshuttering heaven.

II.
I did not go
to the gravesite.
Why observe
another set of abstractions—
rectangle, box, the neat
cuts in earth or
flowers resting
the way your smile would
come and go
when the weight of this predicament
would settle upon you,
that incredible
question that neither of us
has any answers for?

There is nothing really
that I have to hang on to
or would care to, were
it given to me—
a piece of your favorite shirt,
faded and striped,
the old clothing sizes too large—
but this maybe:
the distance between
points, the grasping
in air for a
handhold that fails to
materialize, and this
endless interchange, an empty
waltz
across wide floors.

Is it we who are drifting?

In a way the world has stopped moving.

Denial

We climbed the back stairs
of the old apartment house
with candles.
You were some saint.
I was Jane Eyre.
The cognac heartened us,
but the black sky,
chipped away in pieces,
was a furious red
where the Marina burned
sullenly.
I watched the crumbling
of the cripple walls.
The stairwell was the place
to run to.
Some elevators dropped.
My best friend down
on her hands and knees
crawling toward a table,
or a secretary frozen
by a plate glass window, "I couldn't move,"
she said—we all discover
where the breaks are.
Here, in the nerves
or kneecaps,
where we've stiffened into life,
a queue of ant-like creatures
fleeing a burning hive.
Doorways betray us.
Nothing's sound.
Some of us have missed the boat,
perhaps the point. "None of my friends
were hurt," she says, denial in the tight line
of her jaw. "I will not talk of quakes."
And all of us are buying Christmas presents.
Life goes on
now that they've fixed the bridges.

Under Observation the Phenomena Is Indiscreet

You watch me as the scientists
watch the stars and constellations, carefully
measuring the physical phenomena,
my subtle shifts of attitude
charted
as some men chart the sky
or oceans.
"Here lie sea monsters.
here, the end of the world."
I am, you say, no mystery to you.
A moon three quarters full
means I will write.
I always struggle through the last two weeks
of June.
Though you remain a mystery to me,
I cannot wander far from you,
ephemeris to all I am,
to me these things
unfathomable.

Buffalo Bill

I think of the women
you've buffaloed,
mule kicker,
wild man,
when you show me your gun,
the holster with notches,
show how it rides low on your hip.
You've a carnal knowledge
of hip flasks
and fifths
and you look like you've ridden in shows.
You look as though
you've ridden for show,
buffalo hunter,
you've been known to take scalps,
the dark fringe,
the red,
all those sweet little pelts
and the stories you tell,
what the hell, you say
only their lovers would know.

It's always a skirt
that keeps you at bay.
Under whiskey it's like a red flag.
Girl, woman, wife,
they all sound like prey.
You want rope and a bandana gag.
Mustachio'd cowboy,
you stick'em up guy,
it worries me when
someone fondles a gun
when I'm talking to them,
but I've got a stiletto

that I keep in my boot
and I'm watching you closely
my buddy, my pal,
with your eye like a bull.
You can ride, but I know you can't shoot.

Limbo

At the Sausalito ferry platform
I search the faces
of disembarking passengers,
my shadow cast on bright concrete.
The ferry building clock strikes noon—
a glockenspiel spinning in my mind.
I don't believe in ghosts,
but circumstances relegate you to that sect,
being a memory, and an old one at that.
Searching the faces of every man,
I imagined myself approaching, asking their names.
"Are you the one I'm waiting for?"
The men sat back upon their haunches,
watched me circle, lost as a bitch dog
in that bright arena.
Then, it occurred to me that this
was some old ghost-trick.
Later, on the phone, your voice crooned
its soporific of apology,
teasing me back, again, to a belief in contact.
And I have little to show for that meeting but this poem,
wrinkled, unattractive and newborn.

Blue Cigarette Reverie
New Orleans 1989

Neat
like whiskey in the morning
or the way water slides
into a lock,
neat,
the way we adjust
for high water
(or low)
those painful transitions from
this state to that
this water the color of cafe au lait,
sunlight on surface

Notes from a saxophone

Biloxi Dave 2-1-83

      Lenny

          Lady Godiva

Louisiana Bayou:

counting the animals—
bear, panther, wolf, raccoon, armadillo,
otter, mink,
and a rat—the kind
they make fur coats
from—*nutria*,
you've been thinking all morning
about the voodoo museum,
wondering if you should save the one cigarette
for the next "significant doll,"

the one stuffed entirely with ash,
crinkly tobacco curls stuck
to its head, and
how you will smoke it
slowly.

Exposé

Would you be seen
with a girl like me,
a female with small hands
and decadent tastes?
That would blow
your proletarian image.
Me, moving like a secret,

and all of my friends,
the voyeurs,
would applaud
you, standing with the smooth white
underbelly of your belief
exposed.
Under lowered lashes,
the rumor,
excuses
dissolve
on your lips,
their loss
as easy
as this.

The Quarry

For a moment only
in Denver,
between stores,
when he asked me what books I read,
the face of his gold watch
mocking the moonlight,
I saw how his iris broke wide
(like a hare from the brake)
between lashes—
not really like the smug slits
of his buttonholes at all—
and what I whispered then
was frightening
in its nakedness,
ripping the jaws of his briefcase
apart ...
he will never close his mouth again,
secretly
licking and licking
a wound that won't heal.

Radiograph

Radiograph of a living girl,
her stomach and intestines filled
with barium and sulfate meal
for their delineation.

Her wrists are braceleted in light.
Light rings two careful fingers.
Her head is turned,
and she is in high heels.
No other clothing covers her.
She's bald and naked underneath
this x-ray gaze,
the penetration that yields up
her fluoroscopic image.

Even the subtle ebb and flow of breath,
in her an exercise minute and fluttering,
effects the image density, causing
a degradation of the contrast, the over-
and the under-exposure of the film.

Still, one can see how her esophagus twists,
the intestine curls upon itself,
the intimate folds of every organ
patently exposed.

A percentage of the rays, striking her,
scattered in all directions, creating
a secondary radiation fog,
the dull gray overlay that obscures
even the memory of
the eloquent appeal of flesh,
the color of her eyes.

Clairvoyant

I auger easily these days:
tea leaves' gossip,
cards.
Preparing poultry,
I catch myself reading
the livers.
The flight of birds
writes headlines.

I wore your old sweater
to garden
and spent several days
in your past ...
other lives.

The toaster,
the blender,
set to humming
like crystals.
Chakras
clanking like old pots and pans,
I keep tuning the radio
for clearer reception ...

and babble through static.

Menses

This viciousness
comes on me
once a month.
Medusas rise.
Mouths open in a hiss.
Scylla
governing
with Charybdis.

Pushed into
another space,
I roar:
half-human,
she-devil,
metamorph,
fluid,
moon like a test tube,
precipitate,
change.

Spiny urchin/
sea cucumber,
watery fronds
signal
scooping up eggs
on their own schedule—
busy,
busy,
blind.

Familia

Principessa, princess,
my father the Medici prince,
his mustache like Cellini silver,
eyes green, old bronze.
On the *terrazza*—
wherever that was—
the fruit in those big bowls
made it always the same,
the rest—the *palazzo*—distant.
Famiglia, family,
hammered like a bracelet of silver,
uncles and cousins,
his sister, that jewel,
the *nipoti* lined up with their small silver spoons
and all the doors closed to the outside.
There, in the garden,
strelitzia flower,
his interest on peaches and fruit trees
while the trains shoot along their tracks
like dark missiles,
and the soldiers smoke
and wait for instructions.

The Ransom Note

We are holding your daughter,
and we do not want black tea
or ochre species.
We do not want buckets of pearls,
tourmaline brooches
or the furs encircling the neck
of your beautiful wife,
that white neck like a candle,
the long legs winding about you
as you sleep.
We do not want green bills
packed tight as tobacco, smelling
of breakfasts and leather.
We do not want, even, your severed hand,
the stump of an arm, an eyeball,
a knee.
We want only your word,
writhing on its own treacherous balance,
bare
and lying
and knowing it lies,
nailed to the gray center of the almond grove,
locked in a meaningless contract with dawn.

Geschlagner Catcher 1963-66
Gustav Seitz (1906-1969)

The big potato man,
spud-colored,
faceless, gouged eyes,
armless,
organically eaten,
lost one pec and the tip of
his penis—doesn't need it—
one leg calf-less, the other footless,
sitting barely,
near toppling,
but not quite.
Shifting his weight,
he holds his precious
balance.
Thick-necked and hairless,
we will plant him.
Another will grow in his
place.

mysteries

Resurrection.
Genuflection.
Inspection.
"Fingernails, please."

My knees hurt, my
elbows are bruised
from the back of the pew.
The dense drape of his skirts
as he lifted me—
the black cloth—
his hands were like dust.
"I yelled at my cousin," I lied.

Mea culpa,
mea culpa,
mea maxima culpa.

We giggled in church,
my friend, Janie, and I,
Janie mumbling, "Eucharist"
like when the teacher
called us "vulgar,"
that fat, delicious word.
"Don't be vulgar," I say.
She breathes back, "Iscariot."
The world grows black.

Lined up for wafers—
was his body like that?
Like curtains of gauze
or cotton?
The prayers of the women
like footsteps, hurrying—

       tweezer,
       tweezer,
       Nebuchadnezzar—
the boys whose polished faces
I'd like to slap.
Sacrament.
Genuflect.
Wafer.
God.

Vespers

Telephone poles,
like crosses,
slant on the horizon,
the sea beyond.
Rocks, gulls, lilies —
their stamens are feverish yellow.
Blackbirds,
the beads of my scattered rosaries,
regard me suspiciously.

The gulls tend this brooding.
Mist hangs each morning,
envelopes the village,
winding sheets.
Near the marina, always,
the smell of dead fish.
Matins
      Lauds
           Prime
                 Terce
                      Sext
                            Nones

The nuns are polishing my shoes.
Like clockwork
the bells ring
breaking the long day
into obedient morsels.

The room my brother slept in
is empty.
Sterilized sheets
flap in the neat churchyard.
We had shared toys.
A ferryman waiting to take us

across the river
looks back, winks
as he rows his boat
gently down
that stygian stream
murmuring, slyly, "life is but a dream."
Children chanting
at us from the shore,
"Ashes, ashes,
we all fall down."

Is Invisible

the trees reflected
in a placid lake
look real
specifics signify
lunettes
spectacles for the opera,
each of their mouths an open
"O" to be seen from the third tier
Where are we?
orchestra seats because of the sound "orch"
creating a physical resonance
you are the instrument
even a banjo with its twang
I've come all this way to be lost
one leg is shorter than the other
we walk in perpetual circles
exactly what's not being said
I believe in ghosts, although I have never seen one
perhaps it's not necessary
the way grass bows its head
wind is invisible
half-lives and afterglows
when you cut off the planaria's head, another grows in its place
thus, the hydra
none of the myths is really true
sucking all that sugar up through pixie straws
their tongues are pink, and their lips are blue
it is the suggestion that so entrances
every so often I'd see Dad at lunch
my favorite part was spreading the jam
the marmalade was like glass
only the maid wore no make-up
the way rouge simulates exertion
powder with excellent coverage

I dumped it all out of the small lacquer pots
Dad couldn't give us a spanking
an incredible craving for Kool-Aid
my mouth was all purple
we found holes in the sweaters, but no baby moths
naphtha and vitamins
I've always believed in ghosts, although I have never seen one
thick little whispers:
she had to leave
she was pregnant.
I admired the thickness of her braids and wanted a pair of my own
I heard this while eating baloney, which I hate
several times the butterflies in my jar actually made cocoons
but I threw them away because at the time I didn't know what
a cocoon was
it was only years later that I realized why they sent her away
algae have such a lacy appearance
I've always believed that thing about frogs
the tadpoles were terribly ugly
we threw them away before they became frogs
technically, if you want to be truly precise, we both died at thirty
the rest of our lives being spent as ghosts.

Mysterious Screw

after a sculpture by
Bernhard Lunginbühl (1929-2011)

Donna,
madonna,
woman of metal
and rust
Beatrice, working hard,
mystical inspiration,
metal looped intestine and
noodle hair waving about
your wing-nut face,
you are standing—
leaning,
leaning into the job
on your crowbar leg, the foot
like a single cloven hoof,
your great metal hip,
a sturdy double-bolted pelvis
on a gracefully curved,
gently dividing thigh.
Mysterious signs are
buried there under the rust,
and you carry on the Spanish bracket
of your only shoulder
that strange ladder with
its ten circular rungs
for me,
for me to climb
to
the
heavens.

Mood Swing

Sometimes I wake to silky limbs and sunlight,
sometimes in a spasm of terror,
a mad woman sliding up and down
an invisible pole.
I carry my head in my arms.
One foot is nailed to the floor.
Days are repetitive
scratches gouged on the ice—
a skating movement,
an eight drawn over and over,
the sign for infinity.
Routine horrifies me
the way cafeteria trays do
or large keys
or children.
For some time, I've been
studying
the way the
blackbirds eat up
all the little seed on the lawn
eat. it. all. up.
eat. it. all. up.
eat. it. all. up.
eat. it. all.
up.

Mother and Son

She has brought him here.
He nestles in the hollow
of her arm, collected like
a white flower,
delicate petals plucked from
a subterranean world.
Its dark ebb echoes in
the expectant angle of her head.
What had she heard that could make her do this?
Even now he is beginning to brown,
the dewy softness hardening to bone,
the white crown of his head darkening,
the rose tips of his fingers tensing into a curl.
She will clothe him quickly.
She will put him to bed.
She has done this for the sweet taste of his lips,
for honey
and the newness of bees,
his cheek on her breast,
his hand in her hair,
his wide eyes trusting
before he feels
the secret she hides,
dark and inevitable,
under her warm breath,
fragrant with milk and caress,
extinguishing him.

Three Movements

(on an earthquake)

I. Vertigo

I have a kind
of vertigo
This is why I have broken   my little toe
the foundation of my
existence, I am told.

I fell or everything
has shifted,
walls oddly
slanting, or is it me?
Perception ebbs
and flows. There is no solid ground.

Even now, when we
are gingerly climbing back into
our lives.

Long, jagged memories of shattered
glass, the plaster cracks and
buckles, drawing parallels to
the old irritations,
dynamite dropped in
a still lake
and all the dead fish
floating to the surface—
your great aunt's terrible
alcoholic woe, your horror
of the dark.

The way he bought
the crystal chandeliers
after the walls went.

II. Aftershock

Your own life threatening
to swallow you, they have become
a daily recurrence,
like that paroxysmal atrial fibrillation,
(the clinical name is somehow pleasing)
a flutter of the heart, applied like
some electric shock just when
you've stopped sleeping with your shoes on,
driving you toward
quake kits and telephones,
remembering those shredded wires, the
disconnected arteries to some still
throbbing organ,
crowds in the streets, faces
turned heavenward each with
its private expectation.

We have exhausted every posture.

None of the clocks is really keeping time.

III. Overexposure

I have three
x-rays of my foot,
the outline faint like a
dull butterfly flutter
or suggestion of
wings, a larger luminous body
surrounding
the long thin bones of the
toes and a tiny crow's foot and a
smudge where the bone is
chipped and cracked.

I hang the x-rays in the sunroom
where bright daylight
can find my foot
and wind its way
into the skeleton
and soften it, erasing first
the outline of the foot,
or so I hope,
and then slowly eating at
the bones
until they, too, are quiet
and quite painless.

Incantment

Shklovsky
Mayakovsky
stones in a fen

piling the words
like bricks

>   *Tant fo clara*
>   *Ma prima lutz*

Vainamoinen
Ilmarinen
gubi
vzori
oblik

>   white wind
>   and the bird's heart
>   transient song

Narcissus

for Nanos

He said, "You are searching for the other,
the fugitive other."

I said, "Yes," and with a small pair of scissors,
cut the petals off the heads of all the tulips.

He said, "You are a mimetist. You experience life
in relationship to others."

I said, "I have cauterized the wound."
(Although it still bleeds like a gaping hole.)

He said, "You desire through a third party.
Your love is indirect. It is narcissistic, a triangle."

I nodded, turning the three pairs of gloves
inside out.

He said, "I understand this. We are similar."

I shot him three times in the chest and slid
warily into the puddle that formed at his side,
the sweet stickiness of his heart.

Mushrooms

They are everywhere,
surfacing like spare body parts,
the truncated pieces of some larger body,
testicles, toes.
Under rank earth their mycorrhizas
knit an anchor of spores,
soul-sack white and cottony,
captive angel.
This is the part that lives on.

Thick little digits,
the ones we call 'dead man's fingers' push up the rotting leaves
as corpse-parts rise in a bog.
The cut-fungus open, slick starry mouths on the forest floor,
tongue-like, transgressive, lips sealing gossips and tales.
Wood-ears are listening in the damp gullies of trees—
witches butter, ithyphallic, the knotted heads of morels.
Clumped together, the yellow toadstools glower,
their brown noses wrinkling in disgust.
Lurid, the provocative leer of the amanitas invites error.
The truffle-like centers of puffballs break,
clouding the air with green powder.

And in your sack,
the tender dark gills of boletus tremble like your own lips and
limbs,
the same sad flesh-smell,
the same dissembling delicacy,
while the truth lies somewhere in darkness,
feeding on filth.

Iconic

You are suffering
under the stares of
icons—
Marilyn,
Elvis,
the saints of our obscure
religion,
the one without a name.
Worshipful, you
silently drink
your coke,
nursing a hope
as deadly as corn syrup.
Better you should get
toasted,
slurp up the many acres
of wine and vine,
because maybe then
you would find a way out
of the madness
of present time,
find that door into summer
Heinlein rhapsodized about,
into your strange,
across-the-planet childhood.
He said you could walk into
a bright and
hopeful future.
He was wrong, you think
as you
close your briefcase,
pay your bill,
settle up,
get in your car,
and drive.

Neon

Neon is the fire
inside your bones,
the one that says,
Vacancy.
Stop here.
Great eats
and
Girls, girls, girls.
You are looking for
a star
and you find
brilliance
in those signs
along the freeway,
sparkling
like the diamonds
on some American
dowager's
wrists.
Baby, accept
the invitation.
Come on in
to the promise
of hope intact,
and let us bring you,
take you,
wake you
to
darkness.

Greasing the Skids

A glass of wine,
malt whisky,
Makers' Mark—
whatever you find
in the glass,
whatever the shape
of the glass—
wrong shape is almost
better
for the ritual,
keeping it fresh.
You invent
a future.
Either way,
it slides down
and emanates
as wisdom
and, goddammit,
the gods descend,
perch on your shoulders,
whisper into your ears
about brilliance,
future,
laurel leaves,
and by now
you are grinning
ear-to-ear,
and buying drinks
for your friends—
even the ones you don't know—
and the meaning of the Universe
comes clear.
And you are the goddamn benefactress
of everyman,

including the cute, young couple
over there
for whom
you are going to pay for dinner
(a surprise).
And the rain is pouring
down
like a dirge in a Paul Verlaine poem
Il pleure dans mon coeur ...
but not in yours.
No, you will beat the slump,
jump over the French
in a good old American
frog jump.
Drink the wine,
the vine.
Transform it all.
Head home
across the water-soaked Oklahoma road,
across the planet
in winter
with a blessing on
your lips
and a great love
for all
your brothers and sisters,
whole at last.
And thankful
as the music
turns to talk,
turns to music,
and skimpy sound
from the drinks
at the table nearby
draws you
into the maelstrom

that is mankind,
packs you back
into the bank
of your origination,
makes you
whole.

128 to Highway 1

Souverain right
Geyser Peak left
Italian Swiss Colony right—large new vines
Asti right

ghost moon over foothills
rust-red hawk's breast
Lowry says it reminds him of southern France with the difference
that we are not going to climb up into rocky peaks

Cloverdale (City Fair 16th & 17th of Sept.)
325 Cloverdale Blvd. for sale
two fingers, one to Hopland (right)
one to Boonville
chestnuts like little testicles
fatten under sunlight
the immediacy of knowledge (direct experience)
logging trucks, aroma of wood
our mouths full of the wood taste
of walnuts
an old sway-back barn
leaves—hands turning yellow
peppery red of poison oak
climbing the coastal range
it makes it easy this to and fro
Mountain House Winery for sale Merrill Lynch
sheep in the road
turkey vultures perched in
a scraggly tree
Old Chatham Ranch and a sign to the right
convex mirrorlike shine of
the back of an oil truck (Walsh)
cedar goes by on a big flatbed truck
moss-draped trees

apple orchards on left
Boonville
and "lambs for sale," droppings and fear stink
dry creek bed
no beehives
Christmas tree lots on left
Rottweiler at gas station (begins trip)
grape-picking time, everyone else heads east
Elkhorn Girls Camp
dry creek-bed on right
Yorkville: 945 feet, pop. 25
under a hawk
for sale: 288 acres
Olson Winery on right
Boonville 9 miles
Invest in Solar Heating
"Hamlet" name on mailbox
skunk trace
the shadow of hawk on the road
invest in Genetics, Computer Network

544-0472 40-160 acres Nielson Realty
rough road
Alpine Meadows left
serpentine in the soil
oaks, rocks, erosion
a blistery grass
Boonville: 400 feet, pop. 715
Smiling Deer Cafe
Twice nice
Boonville Hotel
Evergreen Cemetery
trees for windbreaks
and plenty of apples
Anderson Creek Inn
Peachland Road

Frank's Firewood 824 . . .
the Tin Man apple shop
some pretty fancy satellite dishes
Obester Winery left
two donkeys asleep in the sun
Philo: 400 feet, pop. 473
Philo Pottery Inn
Anderson Valley Inn
Scharffenberger Cellars
Navarro Winery
Henry Woods State Park
Greenwood Ridge Vineyards right
Apple Dryer right
Valley Foothills Vineyard
Husch Vineyards Winery left
Mill Creek
Christine Woods Winery left
Handley Cellars right
I know you will write about straw
the precise texture of grass

Navarro: 67 feet, pop. 67
sudden air change
cedars, tall evergreens
timberland
Louisiana Pacific/dark forest fern
artist on a bike (all these drawings) picks his way
through forest
waterway parallel 128
the gradual descent
fog shrouding cliffs at junction 1
Navarro Inn at ocean and a line of cormorants
the way a wave captures a rock
bunting of sticks
a worn fence
Albion: 398 feet, pop. 140

Salmon Point Inn
Albion River
Hughes Llama Ranch
Van Damme State Park
Glendeven Inn
Rachel's Inn
Brewery Gulch Inn
B G Ranch and Inn
1852 Mendocino
Agate Cove and Breakfast
Joshua Grindle Inn
... innville ...
Blackberry Inn
Russian Gulch State Park
lunch in Mendocino at the Mendocino Cafe
Ft. Bragg: 80 feet, pop. 5575
Guest House Museum
North Coast Brewery Co.
Grey Whale Inn
Budding Creek Inn
Glass Beach Inn
Columbia House
Pudding Creek
Cleone: 80 feet, pop. 570
a house against a sand dune
Orca Inn (desolate)
west pt: 90 feet, pop. 1120
Seagate guest house
Pelican Lodge Inn
smells like mildew
Legette drive-thru tree $2.50
tree sideshows
101
Standish Hickey State Park
Eel River Inn

freak trees
Indian paintbrush
Grandfather Tree
Hartsook Inn
Richardson Grove
Benbow Inn (jigsaw puzzles)
Avenue of the Giants
Phillipsville: 280 feet, pop. 250
sign printers to write as little down as possible
(Weott)
you're really moving now
South Fork Honeydew
Founders Tree
Rockefeller Forest
an entire forest on its back
alderwood

ON PLUTO

In the Window of My Phone

In the window of my phone,
my life hangs,
unanswered.

In the window of my phone,
I watch myself,
I follow others,
I celebrate,
I cry.

In the window of my phone,
I haunt old loves,
search for the next one.
laugh,
try not to try.

In the window of my phone,
I gather information
like a spy,
watch friendships
drift by,
sleep,
chatter,
lie.

I power up.
I die.

Lulla-boo
—for Michael Coffey

Do not intellectualize your bliss,
analyze it,
give it style.

There are those times
when everything rhymes.

So simple,
like opening your eyes
in the morning,
and all that life
rushes in.

Like it is

Hey,
face it,
we're all whores.
We do it to get paid.
You can lie to justify
that check with your name on it.
Uh-huh, you do it for love.

The old ones I like best—
old men with jowls
like sagging breasts.
I like the young ones too,
the secretaries with
bright mouths and
snapping jaws.

The little family
pimps you, too,
so they can have
nice things.

Sell it baby.
Sell it high.
Sell it like the guy
who has the jag, the Rolex,
homes in the canyon,
a jet to get around in—
he can have whatever he wants.
Ooooh, he is really good.

On Reading Dylan Thomas this October

I crawl through the belly
of syllables,
of image.
You ride at a gallop,
hand on hat to keep
your head on,
tongue trilling like some naked
lark.
You spit out those images,
smile on your skeleton face.
I hear your bones clanking,
me laughing in the shower
of spittle.

Every word shakes the clock ticking
behind the curtain of
my ribs.
Every spit-fed syllable
lands
in syncopation
while you and your snapping
fingers
beat out that poet's
rhythms,
your laughter the only thing
between me
and all his wounds
bleeding bombast,
beauty
and
fury.

Dream

Field trips
Trying to find time to prepare class
Grade paper
Inspection walk-through
Swampy water at site
Try to find cubby holes to write
People keep showing up asking questions
Lowry arrives
I'm stressed he says
You know I've been odd lately and I don't feel well
Can't you see I'm swamped?
I have all these papers
Why do you do this?
Show up when I've got this to do.
Can't you take care of yourself?
I try to work
Someone says Lowry doesn't look too well
I say, I know
I go to him, and blood is coming from his mouth
Sunburnt eyes, skinny, he is turning into a zombie
I recognize this and my heart aches
I have to save him
I grab his head, hold it to my breast so that my
Heartbeat can fill him
I chant his name to a heartbeat rhythm
I give it all I've got. I'm losing
MB comes to ask something
Oh, I'm losing him. Help me, I say
She puts her arms around him too and we chant his name together
The others come. We chant. We chant.
Soon I understand it's over
He's saved
In a Heimlich-like maneuver a piece of black metal pops from
his rear

This is what was killing me, he says.
I question whether it was really that
How he got it inside
No matter
I... We ...
Saved him.

Last Night Someone Stole the Porch Furniture
New Year's Day 1990

Our neighborhood:
litter, the split upheaving sidewalks—
old trash becomes a marker—
concrete irregularities, vigilance, no flowers.
The faces here all closed as tight as fists.
Chestnuts hang, small maces,
that brutal fruit, the spoils of war.
Here and there a garden patch of vegetables
is farmed by diligent women in cotton coats and trousers.
An old man stole our best tomatoes.
"Look," we said, "next time come to the front door."
"Uh, huh." He nods, shifting shoulders hunched
like an old Buick pushing past us.
Sirens, baseball bats at night,
the clean little clicks of locks being picked—
gunshots, not firecrackers, greet the New Year.

Brain Food

What the zombie didn't know
Was that the brain is not the repository.
It is the glass that holds the water.
And the water is where
it all goes down.

Orpheus and Eurydice

He said, "*Step into the shadow, now.*"

I had six teapots at the table;

one of them was called laughter.

A rose opened at each hand and foot.

I said the rose was in my heart.

Stains bloomed on the white tablecloth like roses.

The tea was thin, pale yellow.

Yellow roses bloomed on the napkins.

The second teapot I called tears.

He collected the tears,

like diamonds, in his white

handkerchief and put them

into his breast pocket.

I poured from the third teapot.

Every word was a tear.

That teapot was language.

He said, "*You have collected these tears from the underworld.*"

He left three for the darkness.

Three more teapots sat on the linen horizon.

These were the reflections of the three under the water.

I found a rosebud, there, on the table.

I peeled the petals back, like an onion.

Inside was a single eye.

He asked if the eye was crying.

I had not seen that before, but now, well, yes.

We both turned to gaze out the window.

Butterflies crowded the garden.

He said, "*Look at the way the butterfly teases the leaves, tickles the rough edges with its thorax.*"

A tray of butterflies appeared on the table.

I had secured each insect with a pin.

Their eyes were like tiny jet beads.

His eyelashes looked like their wings.

Their wings were spread out like hands.

A pattern of eyes gazed up at me.

Were there rings on every finger?

I boxed them and put them into a drawer.

Meanwhile he had opened the window.

He had on a dark suit, double-breasted.

He spoke into the sunlight, and the words flew off.

I lost ten of his words, which was tragic.

He said, "*I have not read from that book.*"

He pointed toward a book he had read from.

It was large; the text was illuminated.

I couldn't turn a single page.

He lifted me onto the windowsill.

"*Stand in the light,*" he said.

I felt my wings starting to dry.

The leaves had run off the trees in colors.

Russets and ochres were pouring onto the ground.

Pools of light.

Pools of shadow.

Tiresias

When I took off my rose-colored glasses, I was terrified.
I discovered my nose and midsection
were much larger than I'd ever imagined.
My heroic husband was bald, and old,
and had married me for my cooking.
My grand residence on a hilltop in the glorious sunshine state
was a run-down Victorian at the edge of a fault
on the wrong side of the Bay.
Both of my beloved canines had bad breath and fleas
and my relatives were all mal-intentioned.
A good look at the national front revealed
that the elected leader
who would be king
was actually no more than a puppet,
that the providers of life's necessities—food, shelter,
fuel—were not into giving, but taking,
that the champions on the opposing sides were twins
and that a ticket to Mars to get away from it all
was out of the question unless you happened to
win when you threw your lifesavings into the big lotto furnace.
But now, over time, I've grown used to these things.
They no longer frighten me.
Sometimes I think of Tireseas,
the blind Greek soothsayer who saw things as
they really are.
Sometimes I think that removing the glasses was not enough.
Sometimes I look to my eyes.

Humor

They used to say a personality was phlegmatic

or someone had too much bile.

Now they tell us it's gluten intolerance
that causes the intestine to swell,
the elbows to break out in a rash.

But you know this:
The bowel is the world's true compass.
There are real things wrong with the world
and *that* is the cause of all this distress.
You had a certain gut instinct.

The mind may play tricks,
but the colon never lies.

What the Poets Know

Isn't it strange how the chosen ones
are always the most tormented?
How a so-called "higher calling" generally
turns out to be a one-way ticket to oblivion.
Maybe the sensible purveyors
of law and order have it wrong.
Maybe the person standing on the median
with the doomsday sign
is really the prophet,
the real bad boys the ones whom luck
and the stock market favors.
Could it be that the threadbare characters
skulking around in subways, haunting
public libraries and poetry slams are the
only true heroes?

Poets,
claim your birthright as the
world's anointed.
Rise up and sing like canaries
before we go down in flames.

The Truth about Lenny Bruce or Rue for You

I never suspected that one day I'd be eating my words
served up in a salad:
sliced, diced, parsed
and tossed down in a jumble—
that I would consume them in bitterness
savoring, not their beauty, but all of their lies—
that they would smell wrong,
taste wrong,
and I would chew and chew wrong, wrong, wrong—
swallowing it,
feeling wrong enter my body.
How could I know that the new life I nurtured
was error,
that the garden I grew was rue?

There's rue for you,
and here's some for me ...
You must wear your rue with a difference.

On Pluto

That girl is so attractive you have to wonder
what she is doing on stage in a comedy club
with her rubber chicken.

ACKNOWLEDGMENTS

Grateful acknowledgment is made to the following publications in which poems previously appeared:

"Dark Parent," *Navigating the Divide*, ASP 2019, *Gargoyle*, 2024
"What Every Girl Should Know," *Gargoyle* 2024
"A Ghost Reflects on the Ninja," *Navigating the Divide*, ASP 2019, *Gargoyle*, 2024
"Witches," *Gargoyle*, 2024
"This Sunset," Gargoyle, 2024
"The Almond Grove," *Santa Clara Review*, 1991
"Foot in Mouth," *Gargoyle*, 2024
"Kato," *Navigating the Divide*, ASP 2019
"POST-Apocalyptic Valentine," *Navigating the Divide*, ASP 2019
"Reveille," *Transfer*, 1987
"Familia," *Camellia*, 1987
"The Ransom Note," *Transfer*, 1987
"mysteries," *South Coast Poetry Journal*, 1988
"Mood Swing," *Psychopoetica*
"Incantment," *Camellia*, 1990
"Mushrooms," *The Impossibility of Redemption is Something We Hadn't Figured On*, BPW&P 1990

ABOUT THE POET

Linda Watanabe McFerrin (www.lwmcferrin.com) is a poet, travel writer, novelist and contributor to numerous newspapers, magazines, and anthologies. She is the author of two poetry collections, past editor of a popular Northern California guidebook and a winner of the Katherine Anne Porter Prize for Fiction. Her award-winning book-length fiction titles include *Namako: Sea Cucumber*, *The Hand of Buddha*, and *Dead Love*, a Bram Stoker Award Finalist for Superior Achievement in a Novel. Her most recent book, *Navigating the Divide* (Alan Squire Publishing, 2018) was a Next Generation Indie Book Awards Finalist.

In addition, Linda has co-edited twelve anthologies; judged the San Francisco Literary Awards, the Josephine Miles Award for Literary Excellence and the Kiriyama Prize; and served as regular and guest faculty at numerous institutions and conferences. A past NEA Panelist and juror for the Marin Literary Arts Council and the founder of Left Coast Writers®, she has led workshops in Greece, France, Italy, England, Ireland, Japan, Central America, Indonesia, Scotland, Spain and the United States and has mentored a long list of accomplished writers and best-selling authors toward publication.

In recent poetry she often partners with *Dead Love* protagonist, Erin Orison.

7.1BOOKS

www.ingramcontent.com/pod-product-compliance
Lightning Source LLC
Chambersburg PA
CBHW020421130626
46549CB00006B/2672

* 9 7 9 8 9 8 9 1 2 1 4 6 5 *